SHAKESPEARE IN FLUFF

SHAKESPEARE IN FLUFF

COMEDIES, HISTORIES & TRAGEDIES

Published according to the True Originall Copies

And unto this impression are added furry animalls of various kindes

BOXTREE

To the Reader

This book which in your hands you hold,
    Contains our noble bard's riches untold.
In which plays historical, tragical and comical appear
    And many characters the world doth hold dear.
Before thou turnst the page and so begin
    This journey of discovering,
We beg your favour as we now collect
    The images that thou willst now inspect,
And trust they shalt not appear exceeding rough.
    Behold the beauteous words of Shakespeare
But now including fluff.

The Names of the Principall Actors
In all these Playes.

Thor, a Chinchilla
Summer, a Chinchilla
Jemima, a ferret
Maxwell, a rabbit
Paprika, a pig of Guinea
Nutmeg, a pig of Guinea
Pancake, a pig of Guinea
Clove, a pig of Guinea
And divers unnamed Degus

AS YOU LIKE IT

Act II, Scene VII

JAQUES

 ll the world's a stage,
And all the men and women merely players;
They have their exits and their entrances,
And one man in his time plays many parts . . .

THE TRAGEDIE OF
MACBETH

Act II, Scene I

MACBETH

s this a dagger which I see before me,
The handle toward my hand? Come, let me clutch thee.
I have thee not, and yet I see thee still.
Art thou not, fatal vision, sensible
To feeling as to sight? or art thou but
A dagger of the mind, a false creation . . .

TWELFE NIGHT,
OR WHAT YOU WILL

Act I, Scene I

DUKE ORSINO

f music be the food of love, play on . . .

THE TRAGEDIE OF
HAMLET
PRINCE OF DENMARK

Act III, Scene I

HAMLET

o be, or not to be – that is the question:
Whether 'tis nobler in the mind to suffer
The slings and arrows of outrageous fortune,
Or to take arms against a sea of troubles,
And by opposing end them . . .

A MIDSOMMER
NIGHT'S DREAME

Act III, Scene I

SNOUT

Bottom, thou art changed! what do I see
on thee?

BOTTOM

What do you see? you see an asshead of your
own, do you?

THE TRAGEDIE OF
ANTHONIE,
AND CLEOPATRA

Act II, Scene II

ENOBARBUS

ge cannot wither her, nor custom stale
Her infinite variety. Other women cloy
The appetites they feed, but she makes hungry
Where most she satisfies . . .

THE LIFE OF HENRY THE FIFTH

Act III, Scene I

KING HENRY

nce more unto the breach, dear friends, once more;
Or close the wall up with our English dead . . .
Follow your spirit, and upon this charge
Cry 'God for Harry, England, and Saint George!'

THE TRAGEDIE OF
HAMLET
PRINCE OF DENMARK

Act V, Scene I

HAMLET

las, poor Yorick! I knew him, Horatio: a fellow of infinite jest, of most excellent fancy: he hath borne me on his back a thousand times . . .

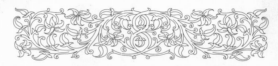

THE TRAGEDIE OF
ROMEO AND JULIET

Act II, Scene II

JULIET

 Romeo, Romeo! wherefore art thou Romeo?
Deny thy father and refuse thy name;
Or, if thou wilt not, be but sworn my love,
And I'll no longer be a Capulet.

THE TRAGEDIE OF
MACBETH

Act IV, Scene I

ALL

ouble, double toil and trouble;
Fire burn, and cauldron bubble.

SECOND WITCH

Fillet of a fenny snake,
In the cauldron boil and bake;
Eye of newt and toe of frog,
Wool of bat and tongue of dog,

Adder's fork and blind-worm's sting,
Lizard's leg and owlet's wing,
For a charm of powerful trouble,
Like a hell-broth boil and bubble.

ALL

Double, double toil and trouble;
Fire burn and cauldron bubble.

THE TEMPEST

Act V, Scene I

PROSPERO

'll break my staff,
Bury it certain fathoms in the earth,
And deeper than did ever plummet sound
I'll drown my book.

THE TRAGEDIE OF
HAMLET
PRINCE OF DENMARK

Act III. Scene II

HAMLET

Lady, shall I lie in your lap?

OPHELIA

No, my lord.

HAMLET

I mean, my head upon your lap?

OPHELIA

Ay, my lord.

HAMLET

Do you think I meant country matters?

TWELFE NIGHT,
OR WHAT YOU WILL

Act II. Scene V

MALVOLIO

n my stars I am above thee, but be not afraid of greatness. Some are born great, some achieve greatness, and some have greatness thrust upon 'em.

THE TRAGEDIE OF
JULIUS CAESAR

Act III, Scene I

CAESAR

 t tu, Brute! Then fall, Caesar!
[Dies]

THE TRAGEDIE OF
RICHARD THE THIRD

Act 1, Scene 1

RICHARD

 ow is the winter of our discontent
Made glorious summer by this sun of York;
And all the clouds that lour'd upon our house
In the deep bosom of the ocean buried.

THE TRAGEDIE OF
HAMLET
PRINCE OF DENMARK

Act I, Scene V

GHOST

 am thy father's spirit,
Doomed for a certain term to walk the night
And for the day confined to fast in fires,
Till the foul crimes done in my days of nature
Are burnt and purged away.

THE TRAGEDIE OF
KING LEAR

Act III, Scene II

LEAR

low, winds, and crack your cheeks! Rage, blow!
You cataracts and hurricanoes, spout
Till you have drenched our steeples, drowned the cocks!
You sulfurous and thought-executing fires,
Vaunt-couriers of oak-cleaving thunderbolts,
Singe my white head!

THE TRAGEDIE OF
ROMEO AND JULIET

Act I, Scene V

ROMEO

Then move not, while my prayer's
effect I take.
Thus from my lips, by yours,
my sin is purged.

JULIET

Then have my lips the sin that they
have took.

ROMEO

Sin from thy lips? O trespass sweetly urged!
Give me my sin again.

JULIET

You kiss by the book.

THE TRAGEDIE OF
RICHARD THE THIRD

Act V. Scene IV

KING RICHARD III

 horse! a horse! my kingdom for a horse!

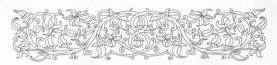

THE TRAGEDIE OF
HAMLET
PRINCE OF DENMARK

Act IV. Scene V

OPHELIA

here's fennel for you, and columbines: there's rue
for you; and here's some for me: we may call it
herb-grace o' Sundays: O you must wear your rue with
a difference. There's a daisy: I would give you some violets, but they
withered all when my father died: they say he made a good end –

A MIDSOMMER
NIGHT'S DREAME

Act I, Scene I

LYSANDER

 y me! For aught that I could ever read,
Could ever hear by tale or history,
The course of true love never did run smooth . . .

THE SECOND PART OF
HENRY THE FOURTH

Act III, Scene I

KING HENRY IV

neasy lies the head that wears a crown.

THE TRAGEDIE OF
MACBETH

Act I, Scene V

LADY MACBETH

lamis thou art, and Cawdor; and shalt be
What thou art promised: yet do I fear thy nature;
It is too full o' the milk of human kindness
To catch the nearest way: thou wouldst be great;
Art not without ambition, but without
The illness should attend it.

AS YOU LIKE IT

Act V, Scene I

TOUCHSTONE

he fool doth think he is wise, but the wise man knows himself to be a fool.

THE TEMPEST

Act IV, Scene I

PROSPERO

ur revels now are ended. These our actors,
As I foretold you, were all spirits, and
Are melted into air, into thin air . . .
And, like this insubstantial pageant faded,
Leave not a rack behind. We are such stuff
As dreams are made on; and our little life
Is rounded with a sleep.

Thanks to Michelle Frank and all the performers from Vauxhall City Farm. Vauxhall City Farm is a registered charity providing educational activities, riding lessons, animal therapy and a peaceful escape from city life.

Please consider supporting your local city farm and help maintain a little bit of the countryside in the city.

The publisher would like to thank Sian Murphy for creating all costumes, props and sets. To Jude Edginton and Jack for the photography and Tony Fleetwood for his photo design wizardry. And Seagull Design for helping the book exist.

Mostly we'd like to thank Thor, Summer, Jemima, Maxwell, Paprika, Nutmeg, Pancake, Clove and the Degus.

First published 2016 by Boxtree
an imprint of Pan Macmillan
20 New Wharf Road, London N1 9RR
Associated companies throughout the world
www.panmacmillan.com

ISBN 978-0-7522-6623-7

No animals died, were harmed or were placed under
undue stress during the production of this publication.
The publishers can confirm that the animals involved were
treated with respect and a trained professional was present
throughout all photography shoots.

9 8 7 6 5 4 3 2 1

A CIP catalogue record for this book is available from
the British Library.

Printed and bound by WKT, China.

Costume, props and illustrations: Sian Murphy

Visit **www.panmacmillan.com** to read more about all our
books and to buy them. You will also find features, author
interviews and news of any author events, and you can
sign up for e-newsletters so that you're always first to hear
about our new releases.